UNSHAKABLE
HOPE

ALSO BY MAX LUCADO

INSPIRATIONAL
3:16
A Gentle Thunder
A Love Worth Giving
And the Angels Were Silent
Because of Bethlehem
Before Amen
Come Thirsty
Cure for the Common Life
Facing Your Giants
Fearless
Glory Days
God Came Near
Grace
Great Day Every Day
He Chose the Nails
He Still Moves Stones
In the Eye of the Storm
In the Grip of Grace
It's Not About Me
Just Like Jesus
Max on Life
More to Your Story
Next Door Savior
No Wonder They Call Him the Savior
On the Anvil
Outlive Your Life
Six Hours One Friday
The Applause of Heaven
The Great House of God
Traveling Light
When Christ Comes
When God Whispers Your Name
You'll Get Through This

FICTION
Christmas Stories
The Christmas Candle
Miracle at the Higher Grounds Café

BIBLES (GENERAL EDITOR)
Grace for the Moment Daily Bible
The Lucado Life Lessons Study Bible
Children's Daily Devotional Bible

CHILDREN'S BOOKS
A Max Lucado Children's Treasury
Do You Know I Love You, God?
God Forgives Me, and I Forgive You
God Listens When I Pray
Grace for the Moment: 365 Devotions for Kids
Hermie, a Common Caterpillar
Itsy Bitsy Christmas
Just in Case You Ever Wonder
Lucado Treasury of Bedtime Prayers
One Hand, Two Hands
Thank You, God, for Blessing Me
Thank You, God, for Loving Me
The Boy and the Ocean
The Crippled Lamb
The Oak Inside the Acorn
The Tallest of Smalls
You Are Mine
You Are Special

YOUNG ADULT BOOKS
3:16
It's Not About Me
Make Every Day Count
Wild Grace
You Were Made to Make a Difference

GIFT BOOKS
Fear Not Promise Book
For the Tough Times
God Thinks You're Wonderful
Grace for the Moment
Grace Happens Here
His Name Is Jesus
Let the Journey Begin
Live Loved
Mocha with Max
Safe in the Shepherd's Arms
This Is Love
You Changed My Life

STUDY GUIDE | TWELVE SESSIONS

UNSHAKABLE
HOPE

BUILDING OUR LIVES ON THE
PROMISES OF GOD

MAX LUCADO

WITH TOM ANTHONY

THOMAS NELSON
Since 1798

Contents

A Word from Max Lucado

One day when Jesus was teaching the crowds, he told a simple story about two home builders. Each of these individuals wanted to build a house. They had similar supplies and plans and identical aspirations. But one of the builders decided to construct his house on a cheap and easily accessed foundation of sand. The other opted to construct his home on a more expensive, yet more durable, foundation of stone.

Jesus explained that when the rains came down, and the streams rose, and the winds blew strong, the house built on rock did not fall, because it had an unshakable foundation. But when that same storm raged against the house built on sand, it crumpled and fell with a great crash, because it had been built on a shaky foundation (see Matthew 7:24–27). Jesus' point was that what separates the foolish from the wise comes down to *foundation*. It's not enough to just *hear* God's words. To be wise and have a life that will withstand the storms, people need to *build* their lives on the firm foundation of God's promises.

The heroes we will read about in this study understood this principle. They came from different walks of life: rulers, servants, teachers, laborers. They were male, female, single, and married. They were among the rich and the poor. Yet one common denominator united them: they all built their lives on the promises of God. Because of God's promises, Joshua led two million people into enemy territory. Elijah called down fire from heaven. Daniel stood before a powerful king and interpreted his dream. The disciples witnessed miracle after miracle. Paul found a grace worth dying for. John saw a new heaven and new earth.

One writer went so far as to call such saints "heirs of the promise" (Hebrews 6:17 NASB). It was as if the promise was the family fortune and they were smart enough to attend the reading of the will. Their stories were all different, but the theme was the same: *God's promises were polestars in their pilgrimages of faith.* They understood that God would not—indeed, *could* not—break his promises. And when the rains fell and the wind and waves beat against them, they found the strength to endure, for they had built their lives on a firm foundation.

You can find the same strength as these heroes of the Bible. You can choose to build your life on the unbreakable promises of God. As you do, you will find that you have a hope that is unshakable. While the rains will still fall, the streams will still rise, and the winds will still blow, in the end you will still be standing . . . securely anchored in the promises of God.

How to Use This Guide

"Hope deferred makes the heart sick" (Proverbs 13:12). A quick look at the world around us confirms the truth of this verse. People today are *dying* for lack of hope. Secularism has sucked the hope out of our society, reducing life to a few decades between birth and hearse. Many believe this world is as good as it gets. And let's face it—it's not that good. But as a follower of Christ, you have a distinct advantage. You know that you have the firm foundation of God's promises on which to build your life. But how do you do this?

The goal of the *Unshakable Hope* small-group study is to provide you with concrete examples from the men and women of the Bible that will show you how to walk with God each day and live out his promises. The objective is to help you begin to change your perspective so you start to filter the events in your world through the promises of God. In this way, when problems arise, instead of giving in to doubts, fears, and anxieties, you will find yourself saying, "This seems bad, but I know that God said . . ." When struggles threaten, you will find yourself flipping through Scripture, saying, "I think God said something about this." When comforting others, you will find yourself asking, "Do you know God's promise on this topic?"

SESSION OUTLINE

Each of the twelve sessions in this study is divided into two parts. The first part is for your own personal study, to be completed prior to your group meetings. In this section, you will be asked to *read* one or two chapters from *Unshakable Hope* and record your responses to the questions that follow. (Note that the sessions follow the chapters in the book with the exception of session 11, "There Is No Condemnation in Christ," which corresponds with chapter 9 in the book.) You will then *consider* several passages of Scripture that illuminate the promise for the session and be given several prompts for how to *pray* that promise during the week. You will conclude your personal study time with three questions to help you *reflect* on the promise.

The second part of the study guide is for you to complete when you and your group meet for the week. After a short *getting started* section, in which you will discuss a few opening questions based on the promise for the week, you will watch the *video teaching* from Max Lucado and take notes in the space provided. This will be followed by a *group discussion*, in which you and the other participants reflect on the material covered in the teaching and consider how it applies to your life.

At the close of each session, you and your group members will be given the opportunity to pray for one another and for those who are not yet a part of your fellowship. Before your group meeting, read chapter 9 in Unshakable Hope: "No Condemnation." Use the prompts provided to guide your prayer time as you seek the Lord and thank him for the many promises he has given to you in his Word. Also take a few moments to write down any prayer requests and praise reports from your fellow participants. Don't rush through or shorten this important time together, as it will play an important part in developing the health of the group.

GROUP SIZE

The twelve sessions in *Unshakable Hope* have been designed to be experienced in a group setting such as a Bible study, Sunday school class, or other small-group gathering. To ensure everyone has enough time to participate in discussions, large groups should watch the video together and then break into smaller groups of four to six people for discussion.

MATERIALS NEEDED

Each participant should have his or her own study guide, which includes the personal study section, the opening questions you will discuss, notes for the video teaching, discussion questions, and the closing section for prayer requests and praise reports. The group members will also need a copy of the *Unshakable Hope* book to complete the personal studies before each group meeting. (See the note at the end of each week's personal study for specific chapters to read in the book to prepare for the next week's group meeting.)

FACILITATION

Your group will need to appoint a person to serve as a facilitator. This person will be responsible for starting the video and keeping track of time during discussions and activities. Facilitators may also read questions aloud and monitor discussions, prompting participants to respond and ensuring that everyone has the opportunity to participate. If you have been chosen for this role, there are additional instructions and resources in the next section of this guide to help you lead your group members through the study.

Group Facilitator Tips

Thank you for your willingness to lead your group through *Unshakable Hope*. What you have chosen to do is important, and much good fruit can come from studies like this. The rewards of being a leader are different from those of participating, and we hope that as you lead you will find your own walk with Jesus deepened by this experience. To ensure a successful group experience, be sure to read the following information before beginning.

STRUCTURING DISCUSSION TIMES

As your group's facilitator, you might be asking yourself, "What am I supposed to accomplish with this study?" Here are a few goals you might set for your group:

- **Discover the truth.** The Bible reveals the truth about who God is, what he has promised to us, and who we are created to be. A successful group wrestles with Scripture in order to find these truths.

- **Apply the truth.** It doesn't do much good to know the truth if we don't act on what we are learning! A successful group seeks to apply the truth to their lives.
- **Be honest and authentic.** Many people feel pressure to act "spiritual" when they are in religious environments, masking their true thoughts and feelings. But this behavior only stunts spiritual growth. Successful groups cultivate a safe place for group members to be authentic and honest with one another.
- **Participate.** The person who does the most talking often does the most learning. Therefore, groups that seek to include everyone in the conversation experience the most progress. Successful groups engage all their members in their discussions.

At the end of each group meeting, ask yourself these questions:

- Did we learn something new about God and ourselves?
- Are people actively seeking to apply these truths to their lives?
- Do people feel comfortable talking honestly about their faith?

- Have I engaged all members of the group in the discussion?

If you can answer yes to any of these questions, you are facilitating effectively.

CREATING A SUCCESSFUL ENVIRONMENT

Leading a group can be overwhelming, but it doesn't have to be. Consider these tips to help you create a successful group environment.

Pray: As you prepare for your group meeting, ask God to give you wisdom in choosing discussion questions, courage in creating an authentic environment, and insight into the truths he wants to reveal to your group.

Prepare: Spend time before the group meeting reading over the study guide and choosing which questions work best for your group. If you are struggling through the study guide or seem unprepared, people may feel more anxiety.

Prime: Your group will be as honest and authentic as you are willing to be. Set the tone for the group by being open about the strengths and weaknesses of your faith. The group will follow your lead. This principle also applies to life application. If you are trying to apply the truth of each lesson to your life, the rest of the group will follow you.

Punctual: Start and stop on time. No matter how long your group meets, it's your job to keep things on track. Make a budget of time for each section of the study and stick to it. It might be uncomfortable to cut people off at times and move on, but the group will respect you for doing so.

COVERING THE STUDY MATERIAL

Design your own discussion. Don't feel pressured to use all of the materials found in this study guide. Select the modes of lesson engagement that fit your timeframe and your group's learning style. This study was written for a vast array of personalities, learning styles, and levels of spiritual maturity, so pick and choose the questions that seem to fit your group the best.

Your group might gravitate to one or two of the discussion segments but not another, and that's fine. Choose one or two questions from the segments that you feel your group will benefit from the most. Don't skip over the section where the group members offer insights from their personal study time. This will encourage them each week to study on their own and complete the exercises ahead of your group time.

NAVIGATING GROUP DYNAMICS

Leading a group through *Unshakable Hope* will prove to be highly rewarding both to you and your group members—but this doesn't mean you will not encounter any challenges along the way! Discussions can get off track. Group members may not be sensitive to the needs and ideas of others. Some might worry they will be expected to talk about matters that make them feel awkward. Others may express comments that result in disagreements. To help ease this strain on you and the group, consider the following ground rules:

- When someone raises a question or comment that is off the main topic, suggest you deal with it another time, or, if you feel led to go in that direction, let the group know you will be spending some time discussing it.
- If someone asks a question you don't know how to answer, admit it and move on. At your discretion, feel free to invite group members to comment on questions that call for personal experience.
- If you find one or two people are dominating the discussion time, direct a few questions to others in the group. Outside the main group time, ask the more dominating members to help you draw out the quieter ones. Work to make them a part of the solution instead of the problem.

- When a disagreement occurs, encourage the members to process the matter in love. Encourage those on opposite sides to restate what they heard the other side say, and then invite each side to evaluate if that perception is accurate. Lead the group in examining other Scriptures related to the topic and look for common ground.

When any of these issues arise, encourage your group members to "love one another" (John 13:34), "live at peace with everyone" (Romans 12:18), and "be quick to listen, slow to speak and slow to become angry" (James 1:19). This will make your group time more rewarding and beneficial for everyone who attends.

Thank you again for your willingness to lead your group. May God reward your efforts and dedication and make your time together fruitful for his kingdom.

You Are Stamped with God's Image

KEY STORY:

God creates humankind

(GENESIS 1:26–30)

GOD'S PROMISE:

Let us make human beings in our image,
make them reflecting our nature.

(GENESIS 1:26 MSG)

MY PROMISE:

I will embrace my role as God's image bearer.

PERSONAL STUDY

Did you know God made you to be more like him than anything else in all creation? The Bible says you were made in his image. Humans are the only part of God's glorious creation with this special description. You are a diamond, a rose, a jewel, purchased by the blood of Jesus Christ. The New Testament describes a progressive work of God to shape you into his image. As you fellowship with God, read his Word, obey his commands, and seek to understand and reflect his character, something wonderful begins to emerge. God comes out of you. You say things God would say. You do things God would do. You forgive, you share, and you love. It is as if God is scrubbing the smudge off an old coin. In time, an image begins to appear. God's goal is simply this: to rub away anything that is not of him, so his inborn image can be seen in you. You are an image bearer of God, and you can celebrate that promise.

READ

This week, you and your group will be studying God's promise in his Word that you are stamped with his own image. Before your group meeting, read chapters 1 and 2 in *Unshakable Hope*: "God's Great and Precious Promises" and "You Are Stamped with God's Image." Spend some time using the following personal study guide to reflect on what you've read.

1. How does God's view of covenants affect your view of him?

   _____

   _____

2. Why is it important to know that God's promises are irrevocable?

   _____

   _____

3. How does this week's promise affect the way you look at other people?

   _____

   _____

4. What does it mean to you that you are stamped in God's image?

   _____

   _____

   _____

CONSIDER

Now take some time to allow this promise from God to take root in your heart by reflecting on the following passages of Scripture. Begin by preparing your heart in prayer. Ask the Holy Spirit to reveal truth as you engage God.

1. Read **Genesis 1:26–31**. What is the significance of the creation of men and women being the pinnacle of the creation story?

   _____

   _____

2. Read **Colossians 3:5–10**. How does Paul connect the idea of the "new self" to the truth of your role as God's image bearer?

   _____

   _____

3. Read **2 Corinthians 3:18**. How are you being transformed into the image of God? How does knowing that this is God's desire affect your desire for transformation?

   _____

   _____

   _____

4. Read **Romans 8:28–30**. How do you reconcile the idea you were created in the image of God but still need to be conformed to the image of Jesus?

_____

_____

_____

PRAY

- Slowly read God's Promise for this week three times: "Let us make human beings in our image, make them reflecting our nature" (Genesis 1:26 MSG). By the third reading, try to have this promise memorized so you can repeat it back to God in prayer.
- Personalize God's Promise for this week. For example, you could pray, *"Father, I have been made in your image. Because of this truth, I have great value in your eyes. This is my identity. Amen."*
- Prayerfully read this week's My Promise as a declaration: *"I will embrace my role as God's image bearer."* Consider what specific next steps you could take to apply this promise to your life.

REFLECT

1. Ask God to reveal anything he wants you to apply based on this week's promise. For example, you could pray, *"Father, is there any truth or action you would like me to apply*

from this week?" Listen in silence for several minutes to see if God places anything on your heart. Consider how those thoughts or nudges align with God's Word as you write them in the space below.

_____

_____

_____

_____

_____

2. Consider what fresh discoveries surfaced from this week's reading and personal study. Write anything that you would like to share with the group in the space below.

_____

_____

_____

_____

3. Close by thinking about an action step you could take to increase your awareness of this promise from God or share it with another person. Write this action below.

_____

_____

_____

_____

_____

GETTING STARTED

Welcome to session one of *Unshakable Hope*. If this is your first time together as a group, take a moment to introduce yourself to one another before watching the video. Open the session with prayer, and then ask one person to share a brief three-minute version of his or her spiritual journey. Following this, read this week's God's Promise and My Promise aloud as a group (see page 19), and then answer one or more of the following questions:

- How did this session's Bible reading challenge or encourage you?
- What characteristics do humans have that reflect God's image?
- How are humans different from the rest of God's creation?

VIDEO TEACHING

As you watch the video for session one, use the following outline to record the main points and takeaways from the teaching.

What it means to have *unshakable hope* in our lives

_____

_____

_____

The common denominator the heroes of the Bible shared

_____

_____

_____

Each of us is made in God's image and carry some of his attributes

_____

_____

_____

The arrival of sin distorted this image but did not destroy it

_____

_____

_____

Sanctification describes the progressive work of God to shape us into his image

_____

_____

_____

Every person deserves dignity and respect because we are all made in God's image

_____

_____

_____

=========== **GROUP DISCUSSION** ===========

Take a few minutes with your group members to discuss what you just watched and explore these concepts in Scripture.

1. What statement in the video teaching affected you the most? Why?

_____

_____

_____

2. From the beginning, the Bible makes a case for the existence of God. But what are some of the ways the Bible also makes the case for the *dependability* of God?

_____

_____

_____

3. What are some things in today's world that make you feel anything but important? How will you reinforce the truth of being an image bearer of God every day this week?

_____

_____

_____

4. How can you encourage others who may be having trouble accepting that God has created them in his image?

_____

_____

_____

5. What is your specific action step to live out this promise of God this week?

_____

_____

_____

PRAY

One of the most important things you can do with those in your community is to pray for one another. This is not simply a closing prayer to end the group time but an opportunity to share prayer requests, review how God has answered past prayers and fulfilled his promises, and actually pray for one another. Use the questions below to shape and grow your group's experience, and then write down specific prayer requests and praise reports.

- How can you praise God for making you an image bearer?
- In what specific ways will you ask God to help you build your life on this identity?

- How can you help others realize they have been stamped with God's image?

NAME	REQUESTS AND PRAISES

NEXT WEEK

Next week, you and your group will look at how God *promises* that you will have victory over Satan. Be sure to complete the personal study before you attend the group meeting.

God Will Win the Victory

KEY STORY:

God promises the serpent's defeat

(GENESIS 3:13–15)

GOD'S PROMISE:

The God who brings peace will soon defeat
Satan and give you power over him.

(ROMANS 16:20 NCV)

MY PROMISE:

I will acknowledge Satan but worship God.

The Bible presents a real and present foe of your faith. His name is the devil. In the Bible, he is a created angel fallen from heaven. The Greek word for devil is *diabolos*, which shares a root with the verb *diaballein*, which means "to split." The devil is a splitter, a divider, and a wedge driver. He divided Adam and Eve from God, and he would like to separate you from God as well. He wants to take unbelievers to hell and make life hell for believers. Yet even though the Bible clearly describes Satan as a living being and not simply a symbol of evil, only a minority of people believe this today. Even some Christians refute the existence of Satan—which couldn't please him more. After all, if people doubt his existence, he is free to work his evil. Don't fall into this trap! Remember that he is a *"roaring lion looking for someone to devour"* (1 Peter 5:8).

READ

This week, you and your group will be studying God's promise in his Word that he will win the victory over the enemy. Before your group meeting, read chapter 3 in *Unshakable Hope*: "The Devil's Days are Numbered." Spend some time using the following personal study to reflect on what you've read.

1. How do you sometimes view life as a picnic rather than a battlefield?

   _____

   _____

   _____

2. How does the Ezekiel 28:12–19 passage impact your view of Satan?

   _____

   _____

   _____

3. How do you live with an awareness of the battle but not a fear of the enemy?

   _____

   _____

   _____

4. How should knowing the end of the story affect your view of today's battles?

_____

_____

_____

=== **CONSIDER** ===

Now take some time to allow this promise from God to take root in your heart by reflecting on the following passages of Scripture. Begin by preparing your heart in prayer. Ask the Holy Spirit to reveal truth as you engage God this week.

1. Read **Matthew 4:1–11**. How does this passage describe Satan? What tactics does Satan use? How does Jesus combat Satan's tactics?

_____

_____

_____

2. Read **1 Peter 5:8–9**. How does this passage describe Satan? How does God encourage you to combat Satan?

_____

_____

_____

3. Read **Ephesians 6:10–18**. What is the significance of each piece of armor used to combat Satan?

_____

_____

_____

4. Read **Romans 16:20**; **1 John 4:4**; and **James 4:7**. How do these passages expand your perspective of Satan? How do you balance understanding Satan's schemes, learning to combat him, and standing firm in Jesus' victory?

_____

_____

_____

PRAY

- Slowly read God's Promise for this session three times: *"The God who brings peace will soon defeat Satan and give you power over him"* (Romans 16:20 NCV). By the third reading, try to repeat this promise back to God in prayer.
- Personalize God's Promise for this week. For example, you could pray, *"Father, you bring peace. You have defeated Satan and have given me power over him. Amen."*
- Prayerfully read this week's My Promise as a declaration: *"I will acknowledge Satan but worship God."* Consider what specific next steps you could take to apply this promise to your life.

———

REFLECT

1. Ask God how he wants you to take action based on this week's promise. For example, you could pray, *"Father, how do you want me to take action based on what you showed me?"* What thoughts or nudges come to mind? Consider how those thoughts or nudges align with God's Word as you write them in the space below.

_____

_____

_____

_____

_____

2. Consider what fresh discoveries surfaced from this session's reading and personal study. Write anything that you would like to share with the group in the space below.

_____

_____

_____

_____

_____

3. Close by thinking about an action step you could take
   to increase your awareness of this promise from God or
   share it with another person. Write this action below.

_____

_____

_____

_____

_____

GETTING STARTED

Welcome to session two of *Unshakable Hope*. If there are any new members to the group this week, take a moment to introduce yourselves before watching the video. Open the session with prayer, and then ask one person to share a brief three-minute version of his or her spiritual journey. Following this, read this session's God's Promise and My Promise aloud as a group (see page 31), and then answer one or more of the following questions:

- How did this session's Bible reading challenge or encourage you?
- Are you more of a battlefield person or a picnic person? Why?
- How did this study reinforce or change your view of Satan?

VIDEO TEACHING

As you watch the video for session two, use the following outline to record any additional takeaways from the teaching.

We are in a battle, and we must take it seriously

_____

_____

_____

The devil is a splitter, a divider, and a wedge driver

_____

_____

_____

Satan was anointed and blameless until his heart became proud

_____

_____

_____

Satan tempted Adam and Eve by offering them power and control

_____

_____

_____

Satan has been cast out of heaven but is not yet out of our lives

_____

_____

_____

Consequently, we need to take up the armor of God each day

_____

_____

_____

GROUP DISCUSSION

Take a few minutes with your group members to discuss what you just watched and explore these concepts in Scripture.

1. What statement in the video teaching affected you the most? Why?

_____

_____

2. How does the idea of being in a battle affect the way you should approach each day?

_____

_____

3. How does it help you to know the enemy has already been defeated?

_____

_____

4. How can you be alert to the enemy's tactics but not live in fear of him? How do you maintain the right perspective?

_____

_____

5. What is your specific action step to live out this promise of God this week?

_____

_____

PRAY

Close your time together with prayer. Remember to share prayer requests and review how God has answered past prayers and fulfilled his promises. Use the questions below to shape and grow your group's experience during this time.

- How can you praise God for the victory he promises over the enemy?

- In what specific ways will you ask God to help you build your life on this promise?
- How can you pray this promise over those who are not yet part of the group?

NAME	REQUESTS AND PRAISES

NEXT WEEK

Next week, you and your group will look at God's promise that you are his heir and a co-heir with Jesus. Be sure to complete the personal study before you attend the group meeting.

You Are an Heir of God

KEY STORY:
God tells Joshua to take the Promised Land
(JOSHUA 1:1–18)

GOD'S PROMISE:
We are heirs—heirs of God and co-heirs with Christ.
(ROMANS 8:17)

MY PROMISE:
I will live out of my inheritance,
not my circumstances.

PERSONAL STUDY

You are not simply a slave, servant, or "saint" of God. No, you are a son or daughter. You have legal right to the family business and fortune of heaven. The will has been executed. The courts have been satisfied. Your spiritual account has been funded. The Bible says Jesus is your older brother and God is your loving Father. But are you living like it? Are you living as a prince or princess? Or do you hesitate to approach God with your struggles because you fear he is too busy or distracted to help you? If so, know this: *you will never exhaust God's resources.* You will never cause the heavenly well to run dry. You will never be turned away or ignored. Understand your place in the family. You come to God not as a stranger but as an heir to the promise. You can thus approach God's throne as a child of the King with full confidence.

READ

This week, you and your group will be studying God's promise in his Word that he has made you his heir. Before your group meeting, read chapter 4 in *Unshakable Hope*: "An Heir of God." Spend some time using the following personal study to reflect on what you've read.

1. How can you live each day from the foundation of knowing you are royalty?

   _____

   _____

   _____

2. What is the difference between living from an inheritance now versus believing you will receive one in the future?

   _____

   _____

   _____

3. How do you "choose" your inheritance?

   _____

   _____

   _____

4. What is the difference between working *for* versus working *out* your salvation?

_____

_____

_____

CONSIDER

Now take some time to allow this promise from God to take root in your heart by reflecting on the following passages of Scripture. Begin by preparing your heart in prayer. Ask the Holy Spirit to reveal truth as you engage God this week.

1. Read **1 Chronicles 29:10–13**. Why do you need reminders of God's strength, power, and majesty? How does worship remind you of these truths?

_____

_____

_____

2. Read **Romans 8:14–17**. How should seeing yourself as a co-heir with Christ change the way you approach God? Why is it difficult to view Jesus as an "older brother"?

_____

_____

_____

3. Read **Joshua 1:1–9**. How did God give the land to the Israelites? What is the difference between something you *inherit* and something you *earn*?

_____

_____

4. Read **Numbers 13:1–2** and **Joshua 24:28**. What did God do for his children? Given that God sees you the same way—as his heir—what does he want to do for you? How would it change the way you approach challenges if you truly lived out of that promise?

_____

_____

_____

PRAY

- See if you can write God's Promise for this week on your heart: *"We are heirs—heirs of God and co-heirs with Christ"* (Romans 8:17). Read this promise multiple times until you can say it from memory.
- Personalize God's Promise in prayer. For example, you could pray, *"Father, I have forgotten again that I am your child and heir. I am a co-heir with my big brother, Jesus. Thank you so much for this reminder and this promise! Amen."*

- Your life will change as you build it on God's promises. So proclaim this week's My Promise with confidence: *"I will live out of my inheritance, not my circumstances."* Consider what specific next steps you could take to apply this promise to your life.

REFLECT

1. Reflect again on God's Promise and My Promise for this session. What truth is God reinforcing in you as you reread these promises?

_____

_____

_____

_____

2. Consider what fresh discoveries surfaced from this session's reading and personal study. Write anything that you would like to share with the group in the space below.

_____

_____

_____

_____

3. Close by thinking about an action step you could take
   to increase your awareness of this promise from God or
   share it with another person. Write this action below.

_____

_____

_____

_____

_____

GROUP STUDY

=== **GETTING STARTED** ===

Welcome to session three of *Unshakable Hope*. Open the
session with prayer, and then ask one person to share a brief
three-minute version of his or her spiritual journey. Following this, read this session's God's Promise and My Promise
aloud as a group (see page 43), and then answer one or
more of the following questions:

- What did God show you from his Word this week?
- In what ways were you challenged or encouraged by
  the reading?
- How can you live out of your inheritance rather
  than your circumstances?

VIDEO TEACHING

As you watch the video for session three, use the following outline to record any additional takeaways from the teaching.

If you are in God's family, you are an heir to God's fortune

_____

_____

_____

You have been adopted into the family of God

_____

_____

_____

God's power alters the score

_____

_____

_____

Joshua faced challenges with faith because he trusted his inheritance

_____

_____

_____

You have been given access to all the divine resources
of heaven

_____

_____

_____

You have been given the same inheritance as Christ

_____

_____

_____

GROUP DISCUSSION

Take a few minutes with your group members to discuss what
you just watched and explore these concepts in Scripture.

1. What statement in the video teaching affected you the
   most? Why?

   _____

   _____

2. How does the concept of adoption affect the way you
   view your place in God's family?

   _____

   _____

3. Why is it often difficult to look beyond circumstances to
   your true standing with God?

   _____

   _____

   _____

4. How will you choose to fight *from* victory rather than
   for victory?

   _____

   _____

   _____

5. What is your specific action step to live out this promise
   of God this week?

   _____

   _____

   _____

PRAY

Close your time together with prayer. Remember to share
prayer requests and review how God has answered past
prayers and fulfilled his promises. Use the questions below
to shape and grow your group's experience during this time.

- How can you praise God for giving you an
  inheritance?
- What are some circumstances in which you need to
  see God's promises at work?

- Which people in your life most need to embrace their inheritance from God?
- Which additional neighbors and friends can you ask God to bring to the group?

NAME	REQUESTS AND PRAISES

NEXT WEEK

Next week, you and your group will look at how you can know that your prayers have power. Be sure to complete the personal study before you attend the group meeting.

Your Prayers Have Power

KEY STORY:
Elijah's prayers call down fire from heaven
(1 KINGS 18:16–46)

GOD'S PROMISE:
When a believing person prays,
great things happen.
(JAMES 5:16 NCV)

MY PROMISE:
I will make prayer my priority and passion.

Deadlines and decisions dot your horizon. Appointments and phone calls fill your calendar. Illnesses and distractions occupy your mind. Responsibilities and requirements steal your sleep. Perhaps you tend to respond to such challenges by pushing up your sleeves, taking a deep breath, and resolving to try harder. When more crises inevitably come your way, you roll up your sleeves a little further, grit your teeth, and give it even more effort. It is only when all else has failed and you're hanging by a thread that you find yourself saying, *"Well, I guess all I can do now is pray."* But the truth is that prayer is not the *last* resort in the life of a Christian but the *first* step in any situation. God has power you've never seen—strength you've never known. He knows no limits and can handle every challenge. He is not only available but eager to hear from you. He delights when his children turn to him. He can't wait to hear your heart.

READ

This week, you and your group will be studying God's promise in his Word that your prayers have the power to impact the very actions of God. Before your group meeting, read chapter 5 in *Unshakable Hope*: "Your Prayers Have Power." Spend some time using the following personal study to reflect on what you've read.

1. How did God go above and beyond Elijah's request in front of the prophets of Baal?

_____

_____

_____

2. Why is it important to understand the basis for God answering your prayers?

_____

_____

_____

3. How does the story of Dmitri inspire you?

_____

_____

_____

4. In what ways are you just like Elijah?

_____

_____

_____

CONSIDER

Now take some time to allow this promise from God to take root in your heart by reflecting on the following passages of Scripture. Begin by preparing your heart in prayer. Take a deep breath, be still, and ask the Holy Spirit to reveal truth as you engage God.

1. Read **1 Kings 18:16–29**. Why do you think Elijah set up this elaborate public display? What are some of the "gods" in your life that you have trusted?

_____

_____

_____

2. Read **1 Kings 18:30–39**. Place yourself in this scene. What would you have expected? What would you have experienced? How would you have responded?

_____

_____

_____

3. Read **1 Kings 18:40–46**. Given that Israel had been without rain for years, why do you think Elijah was so confident the rain would be coming?

_____

_____

_____

4. Read **Matthew 18:19–20**. What are some key truths this passage contains about praying together in community?

_____

_____

_____

=========================== **PRAY** ===========================

- Think about some of the challenging circumstances in your life. Read God's Promise for this week three times: *"When a believing person prays, great things happen"* (James 5:16 NCV). Meditate on the verse. Reflect in prayer on different examples of what some of those "great things" might be.
- Write a prayer listing some of the great things God might do. For example, you could write, *"Father, sometimes you give me the desires of my heart. Sometimes you increase my trust in you. Sometimes you show me a better way."*
- Declare this week's My Promise in prayer: *"I will make prayer my priority and passion."* Remind yourself how you will need to repeat this declaration throughout the week. Also consider what specific steps you could take to apply this promise to your life.

REFLECT

1. Write down a few areas of life or prayer concerns that God has placed on your heart this week. Then write out four or five possible blessings God might give you if you continue to bring these items to him in prayer.

_____

_____

_____

_____

2. Consider what fresh discoveries surfaced from this session's reading and personal study. Write anything that you would like to share with the group in the space below.

_____

_____

_____

3. Close by thinking about an action step you could take to increase your awareness of this promise from God or share it with another person. Write this action below.

_____

_____

_____

_____

GROUP STUDY

GETTING STARTED

Welcome to session four of *Unshakable Hope*. Open the session with prayer, and then ask one person to share a brief three-minute version of his or her spiritual journey. Following this, read this session's God's Promise and My Promise aloud as a group (see page 55), and then answer one or more of the following questions:

- What was your biggest eye-opener from God's Word this week?
- How did you react to the story of Dmitri that you read?
- What types of "great things" would you like to see God do in your life?

VIDEO TEACHING

As you watch the video for session four, use the following outline to record any additional takeaways from the teaching.

God uses special people—but they are special *because* he uses them

_____

_____

You have clout with the most powerful being in the universe

_____

_____

You speak with the authority of God's throne

_____

_____

Elijah had confidence in ending the drought in Israel because he prayed

_____

_____

_____

Elijah's prayer not only moved God to action but also changed a nation

_____

_____

_____

When you seek to honor God, he hears your requests

_____

_____

_____

GROUP DISCUSSION

Take a few minutes with your group members to discuss what you just watched and explore these concepts in Scripture.

1. What statement in the video teaching affected you the most? Why?

_____

_____

_____

2. Do you struggle with the idea that your prayers could be *powerful*? Why or why not?

_____

_____

_____

3. How does the Bible reinforce this idea of prayers being powerful and effective?

_____

_____

_____

4. How does it make you feel to think of God *delighting* in your prayers?

_____

_____

_____

5. What is your specific action step to live out this promise of God this week?

_____

_____

_____

PRAY

Close your time together with prayer. Remember to share prayer requests and review how God has answered past prayers and fulfilled his promises. Use the questions below to shape and grow your group's experience during this time.

- What praises can you share about how God is developing your prayer life?

- What good things do you hope to see God do through prayer this week in regard to some of your circumstances or challenges?
- How can you pray this promise over those who are not part of the group?

NAME	REQUESTS AND PRAISES

NEXT WEEK

Next week, you and your group will look at God's promise to give grace to the humble. Be sure to complete the personal study before you attend the group meeting.

God Gives Grace to the Humble

KEY STORY:

God tells a king who really is in charge

(DANIEL 4:24-27)

GOD'S PROMISE:

God resists the proud, but gives
grace to the humble.

(1 PETER 5:5 NKJV)

MY PROMISE:

I will pursue humility.

Pride is poison. It hampers your relationship with God, hinders your relationships with others, and harms your relationship with yourself. God resists the proud because the proud resist God. Arrogance stiffens the knee so it will not kneel. It hardens the heart so it will not admit to sin. The heart of pride never confesses, never repents, and never asks for forgiveness. Indeed, the arrogant never feel the *need* for forgiveness. Pride is the hidden reef that shipwrecks the soul. It not only prevents salvation from God but also prevents reconciliation with people. How many marriages have collapsed beneath the weight of pride? How many apologies have gone unoffered due to lack of humility? How many wars have sprouted from the rocky soil of arrogance? Don't pay the high price of pride. Choose instead to stand on the offer of grace.

READ

This week, you and your group will be studying God's promise in his Word that he gives grace to those who come to him in humility and acknowledge their need before him. Before your group meeting, read chapter 6 in *Unshakable Hope*: "Grace for the Humble." Spend some time using the following personal study to reflect on what you've read.

1. How did God give Nebuchadnezzar an opportunity to demonstrate humility?

   _____

   _____

   _____

2. How can you honestly assess whether you suffer from pride?

   _____

   _____

   _____

3. When the mighty fall, the fall is mighty. How can focusing on others instead of yourself help you to grow in humility?

   _____

   _____

   _____

4. What are some of the checks and balances in your life to help keep you humble?

_____

_____

_____

CONSIDER

Now take some time to allow this promise from God to take root in your heart by reflecting on the following passages of Scripture. Begin by preparing your heart in prayer. Ask the Holy Spirit to help you put a finger on any pride in your life and confess it before you begin.

1. Read **Daniel 4:1–18**. Imagine you are in Daniel's sandals. What would have gone through your heart and mind as you heard the king share his dream?

_____

_____

_____

2. Read **Daniel 4:19–27**. What interpretation and advice does Daniel offer? How do you see humility and wisdom in Daniel's words?

_____

_____

_____

3. Read **Daniel 4:28–37**. Put Nebuchadnezzar's story into your own words. How does God work through this situation to receive glory?

_____

_____

_____

4. Read **Romans 12:3** and **Philippians 2:3**. How can you incorporate the wisdom of these verses into your life?

_____

_____

_____

PRAY

- Slowly read God's Promise for this session three times: *"God resists the proud, but gives grace to the humble"* (1 Peter 5:5 NKJV). As you meditate on this promise, reflect on areas of pride and humility in your life. Ask the Holy Spirit for clarity.
- Personalize God's Promise for this week. For example, you could pray, *"Father, the image of you resisting me is not a good picture. I don't want to be proud. Fill me with a right view of myself and keep me humble in your eyes. Amen."*
- Make this week's My Promise your prayer throughout your week: *"I will pursue humility."* Consider what specific steps you could take to apply this promise to your life.

REFLECT

1. Think about some people in your life who you feel demonstrated humility. What did they model for you? What can you learn from their example on how to resist pride?

_____

_____

_____

_____

2. Consider what fresh discoveries surfaced from this session's reading and personal study. Write anything that you would like to share with the group in the space below.

_____

_____

_____

_____

3. Close by thinking about an action step you could take to increase your awareness of this promise from God or share it with another person. Write this action below.

_____

_____

_____

_____

GETTING STARTED

Welcome to session five of *Unshakable Hope*. Open the session with prayer, and then ask one person to share a brief three-minute version of his or her spiritual journey. Following this, read this session's God's Promise and My Promise aloud as a group (see page 67), and then answer one or more of the following questions:

- What did God reveal to you about pride this week?
- What did God reveal to you about humility this week?
- What are some ways that Jesus modeled humility?

VIDEO TEACHING

As you watch the video for session five, use the following outline to record any additional takeaways from the teaching.

The deceptive and deadly power of pride

King Nebuchadnezzar's unusual dream

Daniel interprets the dream and urges the king to repent

Why God loves humility but resists the proud

Nebuchadnezzar's difficult lesson learned the hard way

GROUP DISCUSSION

Take a few minutes with your group members to discuss what you just watched and explore these concepts in Scripture.

1. What statement in the video teaching affected you the most? Why?

2. What was the difference between Daniel's heart and Nebuchadnezzar's heart?

3. What was God's purpose in sending Daniel to interpret the king's dream?

4. Why does God say that he abhors the haughty heart?

5. What is your specific action step to live out this promise of God this week?

_____

_____

_____

=== **PRAY** ===

Close your time together with prayer. Remember to share prayer requests and review how God has answered past prayers and fulfilled his promises. Use the questions below to shape and grow your group's experience during this time.

- What are some praises you can share about how God worked to grow your humility this week? What did you learn from the experience?
- As you look again at this session's God's Promise and My Promise, do you have any specific prayer needs for the week ahead?
- How will you ask God to help you humbly be like Jesus this week as you interact with your family and your friends?

NAME	REQUESTS AND PRAISES

NEXT WEEK

Next week, you and your group will look at God's promise that he understands you. Be sure to complete the personal study before you attend the group meeting.

God Gets You

KEY STORY:
God becomes flesh and enters the world
(LUKE 2:4-7)

GOD'S PROMISE:
Our high priest is able to understand
our weaknesses.
(HEBREWS 4:15 NCV)

MY PROMISE:
I will draw near to God with confidence
that he hears me and understands me.

We serve a God who is able to understand us. There is a reason for this: God became flesh in the form of Jesus Christ. He was miraculously conceived, yet naturally delivered. He was born, yet born of a virgin. Had Jesus simply descended to earth in the form of a mighty being, we would respect him but never draw near to him. After all, we would wonder how God could understand what it means to be human. On the other hand, had Jesus been biologically conceived with two earthly parents, we would draw near to him but not want to worship him. After all, we would wonder if he was any different than you and me. But because Jesus is *both*—at once God and human—we have the best of both worlds. He *is* fully human, so we draw near to him. He *is* fully divine, so we worship him. Our God gets us. As a result, we are not left to languish on our own but find mercy and grace when we need it.

READ

This week, you and your group will be studying God's promise in his Word that he understands you and everything that you will face on this earth. Before your group meeting, read chapter 7 in *Unshakable Hope*: "God Gets You." Spend some time using the following personal study to reflect on what you've read.

1. How does Jesus' humanity give you a greater appreciation of his ability to understand what you face in this life?

   _____

   _____

   _____

2. How does Jesus' deity give you confidence in his ability to overcome anything you face?

   _____

   _____

   _____

3. How does Jesus' sinlessness actually help him to understand the temptations you will face even more?

   _____

   _____

   _____

4. How does the story of Sara Tucholsky give you a greater appreciation for Jesus?

_____

_____

_____

=========== **CONSIDER** ===========

Now take some time to allow this promise from God to take root in your heart by reflecting on the following passages of Scripture. Begin by preparing your heart in prayer. Admit any areas of struggle or weakness as you approach this study, knowing that God understands.

1. Read **Colossians 1:15–20**. How does this passage stretch your appreciation or understanding of Jesus?

_____

_____

_____

2. Read **Luke 2:41–52**. Why is the humanity of Jesus important in building an ongoing relationship with him?

_____

_____

_____

3. Read **Matthew 26:36–46**. How does Jesus' struggle in the Garden of Gethsemane help you relate to some of your own trials, temptations, or struggles?

_____

_____

_____

4. Read **Hebrews 5:7–10** and **Hebrews 10:19–23**. How do these passages remove any barriers to approach God with your struggles and increase your confidence that he will hear your prayers?

_____

_____

_____

PRAY

- Read God's Promise for this week three times: *"Our high priest is able to understand our weaknesses"* (Hebrews 4:15 NCV). As you reflect on this promise, think about areas in your life where you feel distant from God and take these to him.
- Write a prayer to God reflecting on God's Promise. For example, you could write, *"Father, some of my areas of weakness have been there for so long. Help me to embrace the humanity of your Son so I can understand how you can relate to my struggles."*

- Declare this week's My Promise in prayer: *"I will draw near to God with confidence that he hears me and understands me."* Consider what specific steps you could take to apply this promise to your life.

REFLECT

1. Write down a few different areas of your life that you view as weaknesses. Commit this week to reminding yourself that you have a high priest who understands and accepts you, and that you can—and *will*—approach him with confidence in these areas.

_____

_____

_____

_____

2. Consider what fresh discoveries surfaced from this session's reading and personal study. Write anything that you would like to share with the group in the space below.

_____

_____

_____

_____

3. Close by thinking about an action step you could take to increase your awareness of this promise from God or share it with another person. Write this action below.

_____

_____

_____

_____

_____

GROUP STUDY

Welcome to session six of *Unshakable Hope*. Open the session with prayer, and then ask one person to share a brief three-minute version of his or her spiritual journey. Following this, read this session's God's Promise and My Promise aloud as a group (see page 79), and then answer one or more of the following questions:

- Which passage encouraged you to grow in confidence when approaching God?
- In what specific ways does Jesus' humanity encourage you?
- In what specific ways does Jesus' deity encourage you?

VIDEO TEACHING

As you watch the video for session six, use the following outline to record any additional takeaways from the teaching.

The remarkable *ordinariness* of the Savior's entry into the world

_____

_____

_____

Why God chose to go so far as to send his own Son to earth

_____

_____

_____

The stunning idea behind the term *incarnation*

_____

_____

_____

Why Jesus had to be fully human *and* fully divine

_____

_____

_____

Why the promise that *God gets us* matters to each of us

_____

_____

_____

GROUP DISCUSSION

Take a few minutes with your group members to discuss what you just watched and explore these concepts in Scripture.

1. What statement in the video teaching affected you the most? Why?

_____

_____

_____

2. What are some of the ways that people tend to picture God? What does the fact that he chose to enter the world as a baby tell you about his nature?

_____

_____

_____

3. How does Jesus' humanity cause you to desire to draw near him? How does Jesus' divinity cause you to want to worship him?

_____

_____

_____

4. How do you wrap your mind around the fact that Jesus was both human and divine at the same time? What

stories in the Bible illustrate both his humanity and divinity?

_____

_____

_____

5. What is your specific action step to live out this promise of God this week?

_____

_____

_____

PRAY

Close your time together with prayer. Remember to share prayer requests and review how God has answered past prayers and fulfilled his promises. Use the questions below to shape and grow your group's experience during this time.

- How did you see God at work around you this week? How did this build your confidence in approaching your heavenly Father with your needs?
- This week, you were challenged to look at areas of weakness. What specific prayer request are you willing to share related to an area of weakness or struggle?

UNSHAKABLE HOPE STUDY GUIDE

- There are people in your life who need the confidence of knowing God understands their weaknesses. How can you and your small group pray for one of these important people in your sphere of influence?

NAME	REQUESTS AND PRAISES

NEXT WEEK

Next week, you and your group will look at God's promise that Jesus is praying for you. Be sure to complete the personal study before you attend the group meeting.

Jesus Is Praying for You

KEY STORY:

Jesus prays for his disciples in the storm

(MATTHEW 14:22–24)

GOD'S PROMISE:

[Jesus] is at the right hand of God and
is also interceding for us.

(ROMANS 8:34)

MY PROMISE:

I will take heart because Jesus
is speaking up for me.

PERSONAL STUDY

Life is filled with storms. But ponder this promise: right now . . . at this very moment . . . in the midst of your storm . . . Jesus is interceding for you. The King of the universe is speaking up on *your* behalf. He is calling out to the heavenly Father for *you*. He is urging the Holy Spirit to help *you*. You do not fight the wind and waves alone, for you have the mightiest Prince and holiest advocate standing up for you. Of course, you might object. If Jesus were really praying for you, then why did the storm even happen in the first place? Wouldn't an interceding Jesus guarantee a storm-free life? Yes . . . but that storm-free existence will be inaugurated in the eternal kingdom. In the meantime, since this is a fallen world—and since the devil still stirs doubt and fear—you can count on storms. But you can also count on the presence and prayers of Christ in the midst of them. What Satan intends for evil, Jesus will use for good.

READ

This week, you and your group will be studying God's promise in his Word that Jesus is interceding for you before God the Father. Before your group meeting, read chapter 8 in *Unshakable Hope*: "Christ Is Praying for You." Spend some time using the following personal study to reflect on what you've read.

1. How does it affect your view of God to know that storms come into the lives of even those who are obedient to him?

   _____

   _____

   _____

2. How would you put the phrase "interceding for us" in your own words?

   _____

   _____

   _____

3. Why do you think some Christians believe they should have a storm-free life?

   _____

   _____

   _____

4. Why did Jesus' calming of the storm lead the disciples to worship him?

_____

_____

_____

CONSIDER

Now take some time to allow this promise from God to take root in your heart by reflecting on the following passages of Scripture. Begin by preparing your heart in prayer. Ask Jesus to intercede on your behalf as you read to reveal truth and clarity to you.

1. Read **Matthew 14:22–33**. What are some different ways that Jesus interceded for the disciples? What are some ways Jesus interceded for the crowds?

_____

_____

_____

2. Read **John 6:16–21**. What are some additional ways you see Christ interceding for the disciples in this account?

_____

_____

_____

3. Read **John 17:1–12**. List some of the specific requests Jesus made to God on behalf of the disciples. What do you notice about Jesus' priorities?

_____

_____

_____

4. Read **John 17:13–26**. Jesus' prayer for you relates to your ministry while you are still on this earth. How does his prayer encourage you in your daily trials and struggles?

_____

_____

_____

=== **PRAY** ===

- Read God's Promise for this session three times: *"[Jesus] is at the right hand of God and is also interceding for us"* (Romans 8:34). Close your eyes and imagine the scene of Jesus at the right hand of the Father speaking on your behalf. Reflect on his love for you, his concern for your concerns, and his heart for your challenges. Rest in his love.
- Write God's Promise as a thank you to Jesus. For example, you could write, *"Jesus, thank you for taking my needs and requests so seriously. I cling to the promise that you are speaking to the Father on my behalf. Thank you for your love and encouragement."*

- Declare this week's My Promise in prayer: *"I will take heart because Jesus is speaking up for me."* Consider what specific steps you could take to apply this promise to your life.

REFLECT

1. Imagine taking your requests to Jesus for him to present them to the Father on your behalf. Write down a list of prayer requests you would ask Jesus to present. (For example, *"Jesus, I have a difficult conversation with my brother on Thursday. Can you ask the Father to give me the right words with the right tone?"*)

_____

_____

_____

_____

2. Consider what fresh discoveries surfaced from this session's reading and personal study. Write anything that you would like to share with the group in the space below.

_____

_____

_____

_____

_____

3. Close by thinking about an action step you could take to increase your awareness of this promise from God or share it with another person. Write this action below.

_____

_____

_____

_____

_____

GETTING STARTED

Welcome to session seven of *Unshakable Hope*. Open the session with prayer, and then ask one person to share a brief three-minute version of his or her spiritual journey. Following this, read this session's God's Promise and My Promise aloud as a group (see page 91), and then answer one or more of the following questions:

- What is a passage from this session that stuck in your heart?
- In what ways did those verses or words impact you?
- What is your biggest need for Jesus' intercession this week?

VIDEO TEACHING

As you watch the video for session seven, use the following outline to record any additional takeaways from the teaching.

The truth of the matter is that life just comes with storms

_____

_____

_____

Jesus experienced the same storm as the disciples

_____

_____

_____

The reality is that storms come to the obedient

_____

_____

_____

Jesus was praying for the disciples as they weathered the storm

_____

_____

_____

Jesus met the disciples in the storm—and will do the same for us

_____

_____

_____

GROUP DISCUSSION

Take a few minutes with your group members to discuss what you just watched and explore these concepts in Scripture.

1. What statement in the video teaching affected you the most? Why?

_____

_____

_____

2. Why do you think Jesus sent the disciples into the storm? How does it help you to know that he experienced the same gale-force winds as they did?

_____

_____

_____

3. How does this teaching encourage you in the storms you are currently facing?

_____

_____

_____

4. How have you seen God do the miraculous on the other side of your storms?

_____

_____

_____

5. What is your specific action step to live out this promise
   of God this week?

_____

_____

_____

PRAY

Close your time together with prayer. Remember to share prayer requests and review how God has answered past prayers and fulfilled his promises. Use the questions below to shape and grow your group's experience during this time.

- How can your group praise God for the way he is moving in your life?
- In what ways can your group ask Jesus to intercede on your behalf?
- What specific storms are affecting your friends or loved ones? How can the group pray for these individuals?

NAME	REQUESTS AND PRAISES

NEXT WEEK

Next week, you and your group will look at God's promise that death has been defeated. Be sure to complete the personal study before you attend the group meeting.

Death Has Been Defeated

KEY STORY:

Jesus is raised from the dead

(MATTHEW 28:2–7)

GOD'S PROMISE:

Death has been swallowed up in victory.

(1 CORINTHIANS 15:54)

MY PROMISE:

I will entrust my death to the Lord of life.

The Christian hope depends entirely upon the assumption that Jesus Christ died a physical death, vacated an actual grave, and ascended into heaven where he—at this moment—reigns as head of the church. The resurrection changed *everything*. If we embrace this promise, it changes our own eternity. There will come a moment where we pass from this life to the next. No more struggle with the earth. No more shame before God. No more tension between people. No more death. This is our hope for tomorrow—but it can bring strength to us today. Our finest moment will be our final moment! We have a promise from the living God that our death will be swallowed up in victory! Jesus Christ rose from the dead not just to show us his power but also to reveal our path. He will lead us through the valley of death.

READ

This week, you and your group will be studying God's promise in his Word that Jesus has won the ultimate victory over death and the grave. Before your group meeting, read chapter 10 in *Unshakable Hope*: "This Temporary Tomb." Spend some time using the following personal study to reflect on what you've read.

1. In what ways is the cemetery a place of *gain* rather than *loss*?

_____

_____

_____

2. Why is belief in the resurrection such a critical part of the Christian faith?

_____

_____

_____

3. How would you describe seeing yourself "as you were meant to be"?

_____

_____

_____

4. How can you "set your eyes" on the hope of this promise?

_____

_____

_____

CONSIDER

Now take some time to allow this promise from God to take root in your heart by reflecting on the following passages of Scripture. Begin by preparing your heart in prayer. Ask the Holy Spirit to remove any fears you may have and give you peace as you study these verses.

1. Read 1 Corinthians 15:20–23 and 15:50–58. What encouragement do these passages provide about the future? What encouragement do they provide for your present?

   _____

   _____

   _____

2. Read Luke 23:39–43. What was the unshakable hope for the one thief on the cross?

   _____

   _____

   _____

3. Read Matthew 25:31–46. How do these words of Jesus comfort you? What concerns do they raise in you? What does this passage mean for you personally?

   _____

   _____

   _____

4. Read **2 Peter 3:9–14**. How can you anchor your hope in this passage when the trials of your day seem overwhelming?

_____

_____

_____

PRAY

- Read God's Promise for this week three times: *"Death has been swallowed up in victory"* (1 Corinthians 15:54). Talk to God about how you can view death as victory. Talk to him about your honest fears, questions, and concerns.
- Write God's Promise as an expression of praise. For example, you could write, *"Father, I thank you for your unshakable promises that death has been swallowed up. Thank you for sending Jesus to conquer death so we could experience eternal life."*
- Declare this week's My Promise as a prayer of hope but also as a request: *"I will entrust my death to the Lord of life."* Consider what specific steps you could take to apply this promise to your life.

REFLECT

1. Think about an experience you have had with death. Maybe you lost a parent, a child, a friend, or a coworker. Describe a few of the thoughts and emotions you experienced. Then write two words: *hope* and *victory*. How do those two words compare to your other list of words? What do you learn in this comparison or contrast?

_____

_____

_____

2. Consider what fresh discoveries surfaced from this session's reading and personal study. Write anything that you would like to share with the group in the space below.

_____

_____

_____

_____

3. Close by thinking about an action step you could take to increase your awareness of this promise from God or share it with another person. Write this action below.

_____

_____

_____

_____

_____

GETTING STARTED

Welcome to session eight of *Unshakable Hope*. Open the session with prayer, and then ask one person to share a brief three-minute version of his or her spiritual journey. Following this, read this session's God's Promise and My Promise aloud as a group (see page 103), and then answer one or more of the following questions:

- Why is the topic of death so difficult for people to discuss?
- What verse from this session especially comforted you?
- How can you look at death through the lens of victory and hope?

VIDEO TEACHING

As you watch the video for session eight, use the following outline to record any additional takeaways from the teaching.

Death is a very real part of life

_____

_____

Our hope depends entirely on the physical death *and* physical resurrection of Jesus

_____

_____

Jesus' followers believe his resurrection is a preview and promise of their own

_____

_____

Paradise is the first stage of heaven, but not the final version for believers in Christ

_____

_____

_____

Our Lord is a God of renewal, redemption, regeneration, and resurrection

_____

_____

_____

GROUP DISCUSSION

Take a few minutes with your group members to discuss what you just watched and explore these concepts in Scripture.

1. What statement in the video teaching affected you the most? Why?

_____

_____

_____

2. What are some ways that people you know have described what happens after death?

_____

_____

_____

3. What reassurances does the Bible offer about what happens to followers of Jesus when they die? What hope does this provide to you right now?

_____

_____

_____

4. What are some ways to view death and loss through the lens of Christ's resurrection?

_____

_____

_____

5. What is your specific action step to live out this promise of God this week?

_____

_____

_____

PRAY

Close your time together with prayer. Remember to share prayer requests and review how God has answered past prayers and fulfilled his promises. Use the questions below to shape and grow your group's experience during this time.

- God has won the victory over death. Where else have you seen God's victory in your life this week?
- In what areas do you need to ask God to reveal the victory?
- How can you pray for someone in your life who is struggling right now and could use a reminder of this unshakable promise from God?

NAME	REQUESTS AND PRAISES

NEXT WEEK

Next week, you and your group will look at God's promise that joy will be coming soon. Be sure to complete the personal study before you attend the group meeting.

Joy Is Coming Soon

KEY STORY:

Jesus appears to Mary Magdalene

(JOHN 20:11–18)

GOD'S PROMISE:

Weeping may last through the night,
but joy comes with the morning.

(PSALM 30:5 NLT)

MY PROMISE:

I will praise God before my prayer is answered.

Troubles come to each of us in this life. Heartaches leave us with tear-streaked faces and heavy hearts. Weeping comes... but so does joy. Darkness comes... but so does the morning. Sadness comes . . . but so does hope. Sorrow may have the night, but it cannot have our lives. This was true for Mary Magdalene. Her world had officially hit rock-bottom when her master was murdered and his body buried in a borrowed grave. Now, it seemed as if his tomb had been robbed and his body stolen. When she went early in the morning to place spices on his body, she instead found two strangers on the slab where his body had been laid. Her sorrow intermingled with anger . . . but it didn't last for long. For at her darkest moment, the resurrected Jesus appeared and called her by name. Mary had come to the tomb in sorrow, but she left filled with joy. The same is true of us when we seek out Christ in our sorrow.

READ

This week, you and your group will be studying God's promise in his Word that while sorrows will come our way, they will never ultimately rule the day. Before your group meeting, read chapter 11 in *Unshakable Hope*: "Joy Is Soon Coming." Spend some time using the following personal study to reflect on what you've read.

1. What impact had Jesus made on Mary Magdalene's life?

   _____

   _____

   _____

2. Why did Mary choose to go to Jesus' tomb on that Sunday morning?

   _____

   _____

   _____

3. How did Jesus come to Mary in the midst of her sorrow at the tomb?

   _____

   _____

   _____

4. How can you learn to watch for joy in the midst of sorrow and weeping?

   _____

   _____

   _____

CONSIDER

Now take some time to allow this promise from God to take root in your heart by reflecting on the following passages of Scripture. Begin by stilling your heart and mind for a full two minutes. Ask God to help you wholly focus on him as you study his Word.

1. Read **John 19:16–25**. What emotions might Mary Magdalene have experienced as she witnessed Jesus' crucifixion?

2. Read **John 20:1–10**. What was Mary's expectation when she went to the tomb? What was her response? How might you have had a similar response to Mary?

3. Read **John 20:11–18**. What transformation of Mary do we see in this passage? Why do you think Jesus chose to appear to her in the way that he did?

4. Read **John 15:9–11**. What does it mean to have Jesus' joy within you? What do you think it means to have full joy?

_____

_____

_____

PRAY

- Read God's Promise for this week three times: *"Weeping may last through the night, but joy comes with the morning"* (Psalm 30:5 NLT). Repeat this verse with your eyes closed, and cling to the truth it holds. Ask God to show you the promise of a new morning.
- Write a prayer expressing how God's Promise gives you hope for today and tomorrow. For example, you could write, *"Father, there are things happening today that fill me with sorrow. Thank you for your promise of the joy that comes with a new day."*
- Declare this week's My Promise as a prayer: *"I will praise God before my prayer is answered."* Consider what specific steps you could take to apply this promise to your life.

REFLECT

1. Sometimes it's good to slow your pace and put things in writing. List the items in your life that are currently bringing you sadness, struggle, or even despair. On the last line, write, *"Father, I place these things at the foot of the cross. Fill me with trust. Amen."*

2. Consider what fresh discoveries surfaced from this session's reading and personal study. Write anything that you would like to share with the group in the space below.

3. Close by thinking about an action step you could take to increase your awareness of this promise from God or share it with another person. Write this action below.

GROUP STUDY

Welcome to session nine of *Unshakable Hope*. Open the
session with prayer, and then ask one person to share a brief
three-minute version of his or her spiritual journey. Following this, read this session's God's Promise and My Promise
aloud as a group (see page 115), and then answer one or
more of the following questions:

- How would you describe Mary's transformation in
  this story?
- In what ways have you recently moved from sorrow
  to joy?
- How can you learn to truly watch and wait for joy?

VIDEO TEACHING

As you watch the video for session nine, use the following outline to record any additional takeaways from the teaching.

At times we may wonder if God has any word for the dark nights of our soul

_____

_____

_____

When Mary Magdalene met Jesus, he completely restored her to life

_____

_____

_____

Mary's devotion led her to stay in Jerusalem as Jesus was crucified and buried

_____

_____

_____

In the midst of Mary's darkest moment, the Son came out

_____

_____

_____

Jesus has power over death but also a soft spot for the Mary Magdalenes of the world

_____

_____

_____

GROUP DISCUSSION

Take a few minutes with your group members to discuss what you just watched and explore these concepts in Scripture.

1. What statement in the video teaching affected you the most? Why?

_____

_____

_____

2. How does the joy Mary Magdalene found that morning she encountered the risen Jesus encourage you to endure any sorrow you are facing?

_____

_____

_____

3. How does it impact you to know the risen Jesus was not too holy, too otherly, too divine, or too supernatural to receive a hug from Mary?

_____

_____

_____

4. Why do believers in Christ so often withdraw from community when they are in the midst of sorrow? How can your group create an atmosphere of acceptance for someone to share when dealing with sorrow or struggles?

_____

_____

_____

5. What is your specific action step to live out this promise of God this week?

_____

_____

_____

PRAY

Close your time together with prayer. Remember to share prayer requests and review how God has answered past prayers and fulfilled his promises. Use the questions below to shape and grow your group's experience during this time.

- What joys did you experience this week for which you would like to give God praise?
- What sorrows or struggles are weighing on your heart for which the group can pray?
- Are there people in your life who are struggling with sorrow and pain? How can the group pray for them?

NAME	REQUESTS AND PRAISES

NEXT WEEK

Next week, you and your group will look at God's promise that you will receive power when you look to him for strength. Be sure to complete the personal study before you attend the group meeting.

You Will Have Power

KEY STORY:

The Holy Spirit fills Jesus' followers with power

(ACTS 2:1–4)

GOD'S PROMISE:

You will receive power when the
Holy Spirit comes on you.

(ACTS 1:8)

MY PROMISE:

I will seek to sense, see, and hear the Holy Spirit.

The Holy Spirit was central to the life of the church. In fact, everything that happens from the beginning of Acts to the end of Revelation is a result of the Holy Spirit's work. The Holy Spirit came alongside the disciples, indwelt them, and gave them the push they needed to face the challenges ahead. He wants to do the same for us. The Holy Spirit entered our lives when we confessed our faith in Christ. From that point forward, we had access to the very power and personality of God! As the Holy Spirit has his way in our lives, a transformation occurs. We begin to think like God thinks, love like God loves, and see like God sees. We can minister in power and pray in power and walk in power. The Holy Spirit promises to baptize us in power, just as he did for the believers in the early church. We just need to be open to his promptings and be willing to move in step where he leads.

READ

This week, you and your group will be studying God's promise in his Word that he will give you power through the Holy Spirit within you. Before your group meeting, read chapter 12 in *Unshakable Hope*: "You Will Have Power." Spend some time using the following personal study to reflect on what you've read.

1. In what ways do Christians often settle for a "two-thirds God"?

_____

_____

_____

2. Why is the Holy Spirit central to the life of a Christian?

_____

_____

3. In what ways have you experienced the Holy Spirit giving you a much-needed push in the back when you need to step forward in faith?

_____

_____

_____

4. What is the Holy Spirit's role in unity in a church family?

_____

_____

_____

=========== CONSIDER ===========

Now take some time to allow this promise from God to take root in your heart by reflecting on the following passages of Scripture. Begin by taking a moment to be still. Let the distractions of the day slip away, and ask God to focus your heart and mind on him.

1. Read **John 3:5–8**. How would you describe what Jesus said in one or two sentences?

_____

_____

_____

2. Read **1 Corinthians 12:4–14**. What is the role of the Holy Spirit in the work of the church? How do you see a gift (or multiple gifts expressed) in your life?

_____

_____

_____

3. Read **Romans 8:26–27**. What do you think it means to pray in the way described in this passage? How could you begin to make this your regular practice of prayer?

_____

_____

4. Read **1 Thessalonians 5:19–24**. What are ways you can quench the Holy Spirit in your life? How do you think you can learn to live more by the leading of the Holy Spirit?

_____

_____

_____

PRAY

- Read God's Promise for this session three times: *"You will receive power when the Holy Spirit comes on you"* (Acts 1:8). Now change the promise to a first-person prayer. Repeat the promise, remembering the Holy Spirit lives inside all followers of Christ.
- Write a prayer related to the truth of God's Promise and the implications that promise has on a follower of Jesus Christ. For example, you could write, *"Father, I too often forget the power that is inside me. I try to do things in my own strength. Begin to retrain my heart and mind to live from you instead of for you."*

- Declare this week's My Promise in prayer: "*I will seek to sense, see, and hear the Holy Spirit.*" Consider what specific steps you could take to apply this promise to your life.

REFLECT

1. Write down some of the things that tend to distract you from following the leading of the Holy Spirit. Recognize the source of those distractions. Reflect on practical ways to change your rhythms and routines to allow for greater work of the Holy Spirit.

_____

_____

_____

_____

2. Consider what fresh discoveries surfaced from this session's reading and personal study. Write anything that you would like to share with the group in the space below.

_____

_____

_____

_____

3. Close by thinking about an action step you could take to increase your awareness of this promise from God or share it with another person. Write this action below.

_____

_____

_____

_____

_____

GROUP STUDY

=== **GETTING STARTED** ===

Welcome to session ten of *Unshakable Hope*. Open the
session with prayer, asking for the Holy Spirit to be clearly
seen and heard in your group. Then ask one person to share
a brief three-minute version of his or her spiritual journey.
Following this, read this session's God's Promise and My
Promise aloud as a group (see page 127), and then answer
one or more of the following questions:

- Which verse impacted you the most in your
  understanding of the Holy Spirit?
- In what ways have you settled for a two-thirds God?
- What is the role of the Holy Spirit in the unity
  of this group?

VIDEO TEACHING

As you watch the video for session ten, use the following outline to record any additional takeaways from the teaching.

The disciples were never accused of overqualification

_____

_____

Many believers today are settling for a two-thirds God

_____

_____

The Holy Spirit gives us *power*, *unity*, and *supervision*

_____

_____

We can have the Holy Spirit but not let the Spirit of God have us

_____

_____

The same power that put Satan on his heels will defeat Satan in our lives

_____

_____

_____

GROUP DISCUSSION

Take a few minutes with your group members to discuss what you just watched and explore these concepts in Scripture.

1. What statement in the video teaching affected you the most? Why?

    _____

    _____

    _____

2. What in the teaching surprised you about the role or work of the Holy Spirit?

    _____

    _____

    _____

3. How does the idea of settling for a two-thirds God affect your view of your faith?

    _____

    _____

    _____

4. What are the gifts the Holy Spirit has given to you? How is he empowering you for ministry inside the church? How is he empowering you for ministry outside the church?

    _____

    _____

    _____

5. What is your specific action step to live out this promise of God this week?

_____

_____

_____

PRAY

Close your time together with prayer. Remember to share prayer requests and review how God has answered past prayers and fulfilled his promises. Use the questions below to shape and grow your group's experience during this time.

- How did you see the Holy Spirit at work in your life this week? Share a victory.
- Where do you need to see the power in God's Promise working more clearly?
- Think about those in your sphere of influence who may not be experiencing the power of the Holy Spirit. How can the group pray for them?

NAME	REQUESTS AND PRAISES

NEXT WEEK

Next week, you and your group will look at God's promise that there is no condemnation for those who are in Christ. Be sure to complete the personal study before you attend the group meeting.

There Is No Condemnation in Christ

KEY STORY:

Paul meets the risen Christ

(ACTS 9:1–19)

GOD'S PROMISE:

There is now no condemnation for
those who are in Christ Jesus.

(ROMANS 8:1)

MY PROMISE:

I will find forgiveness in the finished work of Christ.

The sad truth of our state as members of the human race is that we owe a greater debt than we can ever repay. Every sin we commit moves us further into the red on the balance sheet of heaven and further from Jesus' command to "be perfect . . . as your heavenly Father is perfect" (Matthew 5:48). Heaven is a perfect place for perfect people, which leaves us in a perfect mess. What is the solution to this conundrum? Adding more good works won't help to tip the balance sheet in our favor. Nor will pretending it doesn't exist and giving in to unbelief. Legalism only leads to weariness. Atheism only leads to loneliness. No, the only answer is the one the apostle came to realize when the risen Jesus met him on a road in the desert. Paul came to understand that *all* have fallen short of God's standard. So the only solution was to put his faith in the one who had never fallen short of the standard. He put his life into the hands of the very same Jesus who met him on the road. He trusted in the one who had given up his own life to pay the penalty for all of humanity's sins. When we do the same and accept God's *grace*, our debts are wiped clean. There is truly no condemnation when we belong to Christ.

READ

This week, you and your group will be studying God's promise in his Word that there is no condemnation for those who make the decision to belong to Christ Jesus. Before your group meeting, read chapter 8 in *Unshakable Hope*: "No Condemnation." Spend some time using the following personal study to reflect on what you've read.

1. How did Paul go from being the self-righteous persecutor of the church to the apostle of God's grace? How did God help him see his true condition?

_____

_____

2. How does Paul describe our problem when it comes to sin?

_____

_____

3. What does Paul say that God did with our spiritual debt?

_____

_____

4. What is the significance of the curtain in the temple being torn in two at the moment of Jesus' death?

_____

_____

_____

CONSIDER

Now take some time to allow this promise from God to take root in your heart by reflecting on the following passages of Scripture. Begin by preparing your heart in prayer. Take a deep breath, be still, and ask the Holy Spirit to reveal truth as you engage God.

1. Read **Isaiah 53:4–6**. What does this passage say about your condition before God? What did Christ do to remove this condition from you?

_____

_____

_____

2. Read **Romans 3:21–26**. How does this passage show that God never compromised his standard when it comes to punishing sin?

_____

_____

_____

3. Read **2 Corinthians 5:18–21**. How did God bring reconciliation between himself and humankind? What is your part in sharing this good news with others?

4. Read **I Peter 2:21–25**. What example did Jesus set for you? How should your life change when you choose to accept Jesus' sacrifice for you on the cross?

PRAY

- Read God's Promise for this week three times: *"There is now no condemnation for those who are in Christ Jesus"* (Romans 8:1). Think about what the word *condemnation* means. Consider the depth of what God did for you in sending his Son to die on the cross.
- Write a prayer thanking God for this gift of salvation from the penalty of your sins. For example, you could write, *"Father, it is difficult for me to truly comprehend how much you were willing to do to reconcile me to you. Help me to live in a way that reflects my gratitude and appreciation for what you have done."*

- Declare this week's My Promise in prayer: "*I will find forgiveness in the finished work of Christ.*" Consider what specific steps you could take to apply this promise to your life.

REFLECT

1. Think about some of the people in your life who still need to hear this promise of no condemnation in Christ. Write down some ways you could begin to be an ambassador for God in reaching these people. Pray for God's strength and wisdom.

_____

_____

_____

_____

2. Consider what fresh discoveries surfaced from this session's reading and personal study. Write anything that you would like to share with the group in the space below.

_____

_____

_____

_____

3. Close by thinking about an action step you could take to increase your awareness of this promise from God or share it with another person. Write this action below.

_____

_____

_____

_____

_____

GETTING STARTED

Welcome to session eleven of *Unshakable Hope*. Open the session with prayer, and then ask one person to share a brief three-minute version of his or her spiritual journey. Following this, read this session's God's Promise and My Promise aloud as a group (see page 139), and then answer one or more of the following questions:

- What was difficult for you in your reading from God's Word this week?
- What comes into your mind when you hear the word *condemnation*?
- How do you wrap your mind around the idea of God sending Jesus to die so your spiritual debts could be wiped clean?

VIDEO TEACHING

As you watch the video for session eleven, use the following outline to record any additional takeaways from the teaching.

Financial liability leads to bankruptcy, but spiritual liability leads to separation from God

_____

_____

God left Paul with scales on his eyes so thick the only direction he could look was inward

_____

_____

Paul embraced the improbable offer that God would make him right through Jesus

_____

_____

Paul understood none of us can meet the perfect standard of Christ

_____

_____

_____

God's solution was to place our sin on his Son and punish it there

_____

_____

_____

GROUP DISCUSSION

Take a few minutes with your group members to discuss what you just watched and explore these concepts in Scripture.

1. What statement in the video teaching affected you the most? Why?

    _____

    _____

    _____

2. What are some ways that people try to pay their spiritual debt through good works? What is the basic problem with this approach?

    _____

    _____

    _____

3. What are some ways that people try to deny they have a spiritual debt? What is the basic problem with this approach?

_____

_____

_____

4. What is your definition of *grace*? What is your understanding of how Jesus provided the solution to humanity's problem of spiritual debt?

_____

_____

_____

5. What is your specific action step to live out this promise of God this week?

_____

_____

_____

PRAY

Close your time together with prayer. Remember to share prayer requests and review how God has answered past prayers and fulfilled his promises. Use the questions below to shape and grow your group's experience during this time.

- In what ways can you praise God for his promise of grace?
- Based on God's Promise, is there a specific prayer need you have this week?
- How can the group pray for you regarding the challenge to be light to others?

NAME	REQUESTS AND PRAISES

NEXT WEEK

Next week, you and your group will wrap up this study by looking at God's promise that his justice in this world will ultimately prevail. Be sure to complete the personal study before you attend the group meeting.

Justice Will Prevail

KEY STORY:
John receives a vision of a
new heaven and earth
(REVELATION 22:1-5)

GOD'S PROMISE:
For [God] has set a day when
he will judge the world.
(ACTS 17:31)

MY PROMISE:
I will respect God's justice and delight in God's grace.

A day is coming when God will dispense the weightiest of verdicts: *eternal destiny*. In the apostle John's apocalyptic language, he refers to this event as the "great white throne" (Revelation 20:11). *Great* because his judgment seat deals with capital crimes, not misdemeanors. He will issue sentences—not of days, decades, or millennia . . . but of eternity. *White* because God's opinions are pure and perfect. He judges with complete knowledge and precision. *Throne* because its verdict is final. This is not a trial, but a sentencing. From his throne, Jesus will forever balance the scales of fairness. At that time, evil will be judged, and the curse that has plagued the earth will be forever removed. No more struggle. No more shame. No more death. God's people and the universe will return to their intended state. All this is possible because Jesus already endured every consequence of the curse: its shame, humiliation, and death. Because he did, the curse will be lifted. All things will become new.

READ

This week, you and your group will be studying God's promise in his Word that evil will not have the final say, for God's justice will ultimately and eternally prevail. Before your group meeting, read chapters 13 and 14 in *Unshakable Hope*: "Justice Will Prevail" and "Unbreakable Promises, Unshakable Hope." Spend some time using the following personal study to reflect on what you've read.

1. Does the idea of judgment bring you peace or concern? Why?

   _____

   _____

   _____

2. Why do you think the Lord wants to have a public pardon of our sins?

   _____

   _____

   _____

3. How can having a right view of God's justice affect the way you approach today?

   _____

   _____

   _____

4. How has this study helped you to anchor your life to the promises of God?

_____

_____

_____

CONSIDER

Now take some time to allow this promise from God to take root in your heart by reflecting on the following passages of Scripture. Begin by preparing your heart in prayer. Ask God to give you a glimpse of the hope of heaven to come and fill you with more of an eternal perspective.

1. Read **Romans 1:18–25**. How does this passage apply to our society today? How does it align with our culture's view of God, religion, and eternity?

_____

_____

_____

2. Read **Revelation 7:13–17**. How does this glimpse of heaven encourage you? How does it build your unshakable hope?

_____

_____

_____

3. Read **Revelation 21:1–7**. What does it mean that God is making all things "new"? How might this change your view of your current trials and struggles?

_____

_____

_____

4. Read **Revelation 21:9–27**. Is the coming promise of heaven truly compelling to you? (Really reflect on this to give your honest answer.) Why or why not?

_____

_____

_____

PRAY

- Read God's Promise for this session three times: "*For [God] has set a day when he will judge the world*" (Acts 17:31). As you reflect on this promise in prayer, ask God to give you his heart for those around you who are not currently following Christ.
- Write a prayer related to God's Promise for this week. For example, you could write, "*Father, I thank you for your promise that you will right all wrongs and make all things new. Give me boldness to share your message of grace with others.*"
- Declare this week's My Promise in prayer: "*I will respect God's justice and delight in God's grace.*" Remind yourself how you will need to repeat this declaration

throughout the week. Consider what specific steps you could take to apply this promise to your life.

=== **REFLECT** ===

1. What is the most difficult thing in your life for you to shift your gaze from a present perspective to a heavenly one? Be honest. Why do you think this is so difficult?

_____

_____

_____

_____

2. Consider what fresh discoveries surfaced from this session's reading and personal study. Write anything that you would like to share with the group in the space below.

_____

_____

_____

_____

3. Close by thinking about an action step you could take to increase your awareness of this promise from God or share it with another person. Write this action below.

_____

_____

_____

_____

GETTING STARTED

Welcome to session twelve of *Unshakable Hope*. Open the
session with prayer, and then ask God to make your time
together one of shifting your gaze from an earthly focus to a
heavenly perspective. Following this, read this session's God's
Promise and My Promise aloud as a group (see page 151), and
then answer one or more of the following questions:

- What was difficult for you in your reading from
  God's Word this week?
- What comes into your mind when you hear the word
  justice?
- How does the promise of heaven in God's Word
  inspire you and give you hope?

VIDEO TEACHING

As you watch the video for session twelve, use the following outline to record any additional takeaways from the teaching.

The Bible reveals that God has set a time when he will judge all evil

_____

_____

_____

Jesus is the one who will judge both unbelievers _and_ believers

_____

_____

_____

Jesus will not only publicly pardon his people but also reward his servants

_____

_____

_____

God will remove the curse at this time and make all things new

_____

_____

_____

We must anchor our lives to the unshakable hope that God promises in his Word

_____

_____

_____

GROUP DISCUSSION

Take a few minutes with your group members to discuss what you just watched and explore these concepts in Scripture.

1. What statement in the video teaching affected you the most? Why?

_____

_____

2. How will your knowledge of God's future justice affect the way you approach your personal challenges this week?

_____

_____

3. How will your understanding of God's justice affect the challenges you have with people both inside and outside the church this week?

_____

_____

4. What will you commit to as a plan of action to consistently shift your gaze to things above?

_____

_____

_____

5. What is your specific action step to live out this promise of God this week?

_____

_____

_____

========================= **PRAY** =========================

Close your time together with prayer. Remember to share any final prayer requests and review how God has answered past prayers and fulfilled his promises during the twelve weeks in this study. Use the questions below to shape and grow your group's experience during this time.

- In what ways can you praise God for his promise of grace?
- Where did you see God help you gain a more eternal perspective this week?
- How can the group pray for those "old things" you want to see God make new?

NAME	REQUESTS AND PRAISES

ALSO AVAILABLE
from MAX LUCADO

UNSHAKABLE HOPE for All Ages!

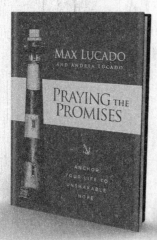

ADULTS

STUDENTS

KIDS

Bring UNSHAKABLE HOPE
to your entire church!

The Unshakable Hope 12-week church campaign equips adults, students, and children of all ages to drop anchor into the promises God made to his people throughout Scripture.

The church campaign kit includes:

- *Unshakable Hope* book
- *Unshakable Hope Study Guide*
- *Unshakable Hope Video Study* DVD
- *Praying the Promises* book
- *Unshakable Hope Promise Book: Student Edition*
- *God Always Keeps His Promises: Unshakable Hope for Kids*
- *Unshakable Hope Children's Curriculum* CD-ROM (12 lessons each for preschool, early elementary, and later elementary)
- Customizable promotional resources

Visit MaxLucado.com

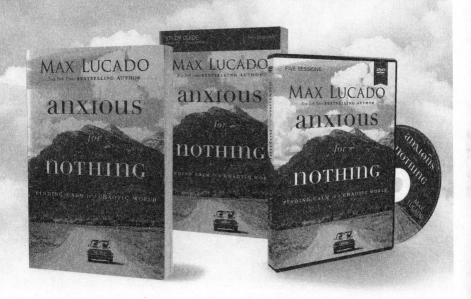

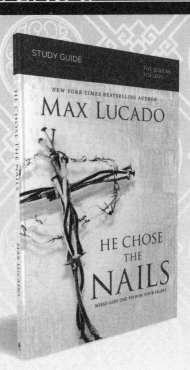

*I*n *Because of Bethlehem*, Max Lucado takes small groups through four video sessions that explore how the One who made everything chose to make himself nothing and come into our world. In *He Chose the Nails*, Max leads groups through five sessions that unpack the promises of the cross and all the gifts that Jesus gave at his crucifixion. These studies are perfect for groups who want to explore more about Christ during the Advent and Lenten seasons.